9/06

First Facts™

Our Government

Voting in Elections

by Terri DeGezelle

Consultant:
Shirley Tabata Ponomareff, Editor
League of Women Voters
Washington, D.C.

Capstone
press

Mankato, Minnesota

First Facts is published by Capstone Press,
151 Good Counsel Drive, P.O. Box 669, Mankato, Minnesota 56002.
www.capstonepress.com

Library of Congress Cataloging-in-Publication Data
DeGezelle, Terri, 1955–
    Voting in elections / by Terri DeGezelle.
    p. cm.—(First facts: our government)
    Includes bibliographical references and index.
    ISBN 0-7368-3687-X (hardcover)
    ISBN 0-7368-5155-0 (paperback)
    1. Elections—United States—Juvenile literature. 2. Voting—United States—Juvenile literature.
I. Title. II. First facts. Our government.
JK1978.D44 2005
324.6'5—dc22   2004011898

Summary: Explains democracy as a form of government and how to vote in U.S. elections.
    Includes information on the history of voting rights.

Editorial Credits
Christine Peterson, editor; Jennifer Bergstrom, set designer; Enoch Peterson, book designer;
    Jo Miller, photo researcher; Scott Thoms, photo editor

Photo Credits
Bruce Coleman Inc./Keith Gunnar, 6
Capstone Press/Karon Dubke, cover
Corbis, 8, 9; Brooks Kraft, 7; Joseph Sohm/Visions of America, 20; Kim Kulish, 17; Reuters, 13
Getty Images Inc., 5; Don Murray, 15; Douglas Tesner, 18–19; Justin Sullivan, 16
Jim West, 14
Photo Researchers Inc./Chromosohm/Joseph Sohm, 10–11

1 2 3 4 5 6 10 09 08 07 06 05

Table of Contents

The Right to Vote

The U.S. government is a **democracy**. In a democracy, people have the right to choose their leaders. On **Election** Day, **citizens** vote to choose leaders for their city, state, and country. Voting makes people a part of government.

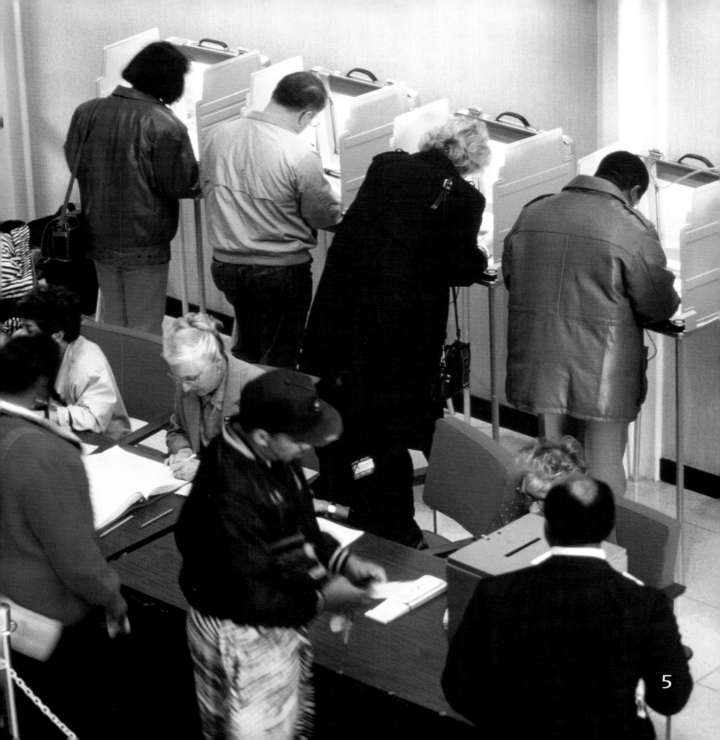

People Elect Leaders

Citizens elect leaders for national, state, and city governments. Most leaders serve terms that last two, four, or six years.

In the United States, citizens choose a president every four years. The president leads the entire country.

Years ago, many U.S. citizens were not allowed to vote. Only white men who owned land could vote. Some people believed this was not fair.

For years, other people worked hard
to win voting rights. In 1870, African
American men won the right to vote.
In 1920, all women won voting rights.

Who Can Vote

The U.S. government and the states make rules for voters. Today, people must be U.S. citizens to vote. They must be at least 18 years old. In most states, citizens must **register**, or sign up to vote.

Fact!
North Dakota is the only U.S. state where people do not have to register to vote.

Informed Voters

Before voting, people learn about **candidates**. People listen to candidates' plans and ideas. Citizens vote for the candidate they feel will do the best job. Learning about candidates helps people choose good leaders.

Fact!
In the United States, most voters learn about candidates from TV and newspapers.

13

Where Citizens Vote

Citizens vote at **polling places**.
Polling places can be schools, city halls,
fire stations, or other public places.

Workers at polling places help voters
and answer questions. Workers hand
out **ballots**. They make sure each
person votes only one time.

How Citizens Vote

People use ballots to vote. Ballots list candidates in the election. Citizens vote by putting a mark next to the name of one candidate for each office.

People mark ballots in private. Their votes are kept secret. Some voters can't go to polling places. They use **absentee** ballots to vote. They mail in these ballots.

Counting the Votes

When the election is over, votes are counted. Votes can be counted by hand. Some places also use computers to count votes. In all elections except for U.S. president, the person with the most votes wins.

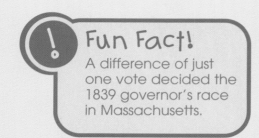

Fun Fact!
A difference of just one vote decided the 1839 governor's race in Massachusetts.

Amazing but True!

A candidate for U.S. president can get the most votes, but still lose the election. The president is actually chosen by the 538 members of the Electoral College called electors. States with more people have more electors. The candidate who gets the most citizen votes usually wins all of the Electoral College votes from that state. In a close election, a candidate can lose the citizen vote, but become president by winning the most electoral votes.

Hands On: Elect a Leader

People vote in elections to choose leaders. Hold an election with your friends to choose a "Leader of the Day."

What You Need
a group of friends
pencil
paper
box

What You Do

1. Choose two friends to be the candidates.
2. Each candidate then tells the group what he or she would do as "Leader of the Day."
3. Have your friends vote by writing the name of one candidate on a piece of paper.
4. Ask your friends to fold their ballots and place them in a box.
5. After everyone has voted, count all the votes.
6. The candidate who gets the most votes becomes the "Leader of the Day."

Glossary

absentee (AB-suhn-tee)—given by someone who is not present

ballot (BAL-uht)—a punch card, piece of paper, or electronic screen on which a person's vote is recorded

candidate (KAN-di-date)—a person who runs for office, such as president

citizen (SIT-i-zuhn)—a member of a country, state, or city who has the right to live there

democracy (di-MOK-ruh-see)—a government in which people choose their leaders by voting

election (i-LEK-shuhn)—the process of choosing someone or deciding something by voting

polling place (POHL-ing PLAYSS)—the place where people vote in an election

register (REJ-uh-stur)—to enter a voter's name on an official list

Read More

Christelow, Eileen. *Vote!* New York: Clarion Books, 2003.

Hamilton, John. *Voting in an Election.* Government in Action! Edina, Minn.: Abdo, 2004.

Murphy, Patricia J. *Voting and Elections.* Let's See Library. Our Nation. Minneapolis: Compass Point Books, 2002.

Internet Sites

FactHound offers a safe, fun way to find Internet sites related to this book. All of the sites on FactHound have been researched by our staff.

Here's how:
1. Visit *www.facthound.com*
2. Type in this special code **073683687X** for age-appropriate sites. Or enter a search word related to this book for a more general search.
3. Click on the **Fetch It** button.

FactHound will fetch the best sites for you!

Index